BE THE CEO OF YOUR LIFE AS WELL AS YOUR BUSINESS©

FITPRENEUR

HOW TO SEAMLESSLY ACHIEVE HEALTH, WEALTH & A POSITIVE MINDSET
WITH WINNING WEEKS©, MASTERFUL MONTHS & REMARKABLE YEARS

HEALTHY, WEALTHY & WISE

By best selling author & high performance expert
NIKKI FOGDEN-MOORE

UPDATED 2023

The Ultimate Leader
Healthy, Wealthy & Wise

HOW TO BE THE CEO OF YOUR BUSINESS AND YOUR LIFE

Also published by Nikki Fogden-Moore
VITALITY, THE WAKE UP WORKOUT,
AND RADICAL SELF BELIEF

Copyright © 2016 Nikki Fogden-Moore.
The Vitality Coach, The Vitality Bank are registered trademarks
Cover image by Janneke Storm with thanks to Kit and Ace
Cover design and Book design by Nikki Fogden-Moore and Amy Tejada
Author photographs by Ashley Streff and Janneke Storm

All rights reserved. No part of this book may be used or reproduced by any means, graphic, electronic, or mechanical, including photocopying, recording, taping or by any information storage retrieval system without the written permission of the author except in the case of brief quotations embodied in critical articles and reviews.

Because of the dynamic nature of the Internet, any web addresses or links contained in this book may have changed since publication and may no longer be valid. The views expressed in this work are solely those of the author and do not necessarily reflect the views of the publisher, and the publisher hereby disclaims any responsibility for them.

ISBN: 978-0-9876196-3-1

Print information available on the last page.

UPDATED 2023

JOIN MY FREE BLOG AND MONDAY MOJO©
FOR INSPIRATION, TIPS, TOOLS, WORKSHEETS AND MORE.

COME JOIN ME ON SOCIALS

@NFOGDENMOORE

WWW.NIKKIFOGDENMOORE.COM

Acknowledgement

I'm writing the intro to this book 30,000 feet above the ocean— on my way back from LA and Aspen. I know that in 48 hours this entire manuscript has to go into the editor for a final proof read and then we need to press play (or in other words, design and print).

Books don't happen over night. I'm always grateful to those who have been there from the beginning, to my friends, supporters and those who challenge my non-conforming approach. Special thanks to my incredible clients who make this all so worth while and to my parents, Ann and Trevor—who pushed me to think outside the box from day one and who gave me the incredible gift of blending wellbeing with hard work and success.

We pay it forward with this book and provide free mentoring and workshops annually for future leaders who are setting up their businesses. Supporting young women and men, to achieve their dreams with financial grants and mentoring across all walks of life. As Warrant Buffet once famously said "Someone is sitting in the shade today because someone planted a tree a long time ago". I hope you enjoy my view on how we can each lead in business and in life, and be true Fitpreneurs for now and into the future.

Contents

Foreword ix
About This Book xv
Chapter 1 Defining The Ultimate Leader:
   What (Or Who) Is A Fitpreneur 1
Chapter 2 Checks And Balances: Where Do You Sit 13
Chapter 3 What Do You Value The Most 29
Chapter 4 Goal Setting: Not Just Another To Do List 47
Chapter 5 Bringing It All Together 59
Chapter 6 Leading Others 85
Chapter 7 The Adjust And Review 95
Chapter 8 Finding Your Dream Team: Strength In Numbers 107
Chapter 9 Enjoy The Journey 117
About The Author 159
Endnotes 160
The Niktionary and Resources 161
References and Resources 163

Foreword

If I had to use one word to describe Nikki, it would be 'Wow". Nikki brings an amazing amount of energy and enthusiasm to everything she does and backs it up with solid useful advice.

This book is no different. This book is the game changer for finding the alignment between your business and your life that allows you to show up with authenticity, congruence and of course as Nikki describes it, *Ultimate Vitality.* Having worked with 1000's of leaders across the globe I can tell you that every entrepreneur, every business owner, every CEO and for that matter every leader should devour this book. Its the missing piece of the puzzle thats allows you to be brilliant, outstanding and remarkable.

Nikki walks her talk! She is the energiser bunny behind a very successful career and business. She can raise the levels of energy and enthusiasm in a room, simply by stepping into it. She has a remarkable ability to see it exactly as it is and raise the bar on what it can be.

If you want to play a bigger game, own how you show up, thrive rather than survive, this book is for you. If you want to bring a vivacious exuberance to the business you are in, this book is for you. If you want to live a life full of vivacity, endurance strength and stamina, this book is where you will find it.

This book is an investment in you. The ultimate investment anyone can make is the investment in their own health and wellbeing as that is the foundation from which resourcefulness and abundance grows. Its the path to being healthy wealthy and wise!

Rowdy McLean
International keynote Speaker
Author: Play a Bigger Game—how to achieve more, be more, do more and have more.

"TO MASTER ULTIMATE SUCCESS, WE MUST LEARN TO BE THE CEO OF OUR LIFE AS WELL AS OUR BUSINESS."

NIKKI FOGDEN MOORE

About This Book

Hi, so you picked up my book. Great news. Welcome.
I'm looking forward to getting to know you and helping you get to know yourself during the next 9 chapters.

This book is for the game changers. The leaders.
The entrepreneurs. The people who do things with life. Not just CEOs of large corporations, but anyone who runs a business any size. It's for those of you who want to be the CEO of your life, as well as your business.

A person like yourself, who gives it all, who is a proud leader at home and in your career.

It wasn't written overnight or a long weekend or even in a year. It's from a culmination of many, many years coaching, working in international business myself and running tailored programs with extremely driven, high achievers who were looking for that little piece of magic to make their personal and their business success a little more seamless.

I call it Ultimate Vitality.

Less struggle, more strive. Less hard work and more energy to work hard at what you love in all areas of life. Less internal negotiation, more clarity and conviction.

An aura of ultimate leadership. One where you are healthy, wealthy and wise.

The important point, before we hop on this practical journey together, is that everyone is a leader. We must lead in life and in business. We lead others whether we realise it or not.

We influence ourselves and others around us. Our actions determine our future and the path along the way.

So—why this book and what could you possibly need to be even more successful?

Chances are you're smart, pretty awesome at what you do and feel that you do excel in business, yet perhaps there's just that tiny bit missing?

That inner balance, that seamlessness that is the difference between enjoyment, vitality, a sense of energy, intelligence and working hard—or feeling that everything is 'hard work'.

Perhaps you picked up FITPRENEUR because you want to unlock that magic ingredient—that tiny tipping point to find the real blend of business and personal vitality—seamlessly.

Well that's great news as this book is designed specifically to help you do that—to find your leadership for business and life, your vitality for healthy, wealth and wisdom—without throwing everything up side down.

This is not a quick-fix, self-help, read-but-don't-action book. It's the wake-up call to what you've been missing. It's the reminder of how simple taking control of your life can be. It is the how-to of adopting the very best habits you can to create truly remarkable results.

It's not going to be littered with statistics and pages of recent studies showing the importance of personal wellbeing with commercial success and decision making. We already know that this is a crucial combination.

Where do we fall down on achieving this? What stories in our heads prevent us from that perfect blend of business and personal vitality. Why do we stop doing the work on ourselves as we are busy working?

Furthermore, how can we expect those in our companies, our families and in our community to work well together and contribute to a successful society if as leaders we are not practicing what we preach?

If it's so simple why isn't everyone a Fitpreneur?

The good news is I am here to show you how it is so easy to put things back into perspective daily. This book is designed to help you reconnect with your why and your sense of purpose as a leader. To lead from within, lead by example and then lead others around you.

To be a true Fitpreneur. Healthy, wealthy and wise.

I coach, present and write on this topic EVERY DAY. It is my life, my personal mission to work with very successful highly driven people and help them find the toolkit that enables commercial and personal success—without sacrificing one for the other.

We will rediscover what you value most, tap into a new perspective—a non-negotiating mindset and find your next level energy for greater business results with a sense of balance, peace and wisdom within.

If you value quality in life and quality of life, you want to lead yourself and others to create a sustainable successful business and not burn out in the process. Then this is for you.

This book is designed so you get me as your coach as you read and do the work.

I understand the pressures and responsibilities you face. Great people never stop learning. Great leaders never stop evolving and progressing to be their personal best and create a legacy for those around them.

I hope this helps you in more ways than you could have ever imagined and that what you learn here you can influence and create impact with your teams and your family too.

Welcome to the ultimate in leadership—finding your Fitpreneur.

Your Coach

Nikki

"CHOOSE
YOUR MISSION—
YOUR LIFE IS
WORTH A NOBLE
MOTIVE."

NIKKI FOGDEN-MOORE

LET'S GET STARTED...

CHAPTER 1

DEFINING THE ULTIMATE LEADER:
WHAT (OR WHO) IS A FITPRENEUR

"FITPRENEUR—
A PERSON OR LEADER
WHO SEAMLESSLY
BLENDS PERSONAL
AND BUSINESS VITALITY
FOR SUSTAINABLE
SUCCESS—A CEO
OF LIFE—THEY ARE
HEALTHY, WEALTHY
AND WISE."

NIKKI FOGDEN-MOORE

CHAPTER 1

Setting goals and working on it in only one direction is like going around the lake in a row boat with only one oar.

We need balance, it's a beautiful realisation when you bring both your personal and commercial success together with equal importance. It just surprises me that so many wonderful, intelligent, charismatic and talented leaders find that the most challenging aspect of all.

Seventy-six per cent of CEOs agree that business success will be redefined by more than just financial profit[1]. Yet so many struggle to actually achieve and maintain that.

This chapter is short and sweet. It's purely to set the scene to let you know that making an audible change in your life as a leader isn't difficult. Realisation and changes can happen in an instant. It's getting rid of old roadblocks and creating a seamless pathway that makes it stick.

The most important place to start is to throw out the myth of work life balance. To me the ultimate vitality and success when you love what you do is a work life BLEND.

HEALTHY | WEALTHY | WISE

The Ultimate Leader is healthy, wealthy and wise. These leaders are the CEOs, the business owners, the start-ups, the entrepreneurs, the managers and the directors who have a sense of energy, are well presented, mentally agile and dynamic— professionally and personally. Most importantly this is all sustainable energy, financial and a mindfulness for success.

A Fitpreneur has their mojo sorted—they have seemingly effortless energy and an infectious drive for both business and life.

Before we go on—DO NOT confuse an abundance of energy and enormous full schedule for a lack of intelligence and direction. We unlock an incredible power within when we combine our inner self with our greatest skills.

This problem is there's no straight forward 'box' or title to put someone in who is living this kind of vision, vitality and wisdom daily. People don't trust it. They think "just watch—they'll crash and burn at some stage".

Can you think of anyone who inspires you by demonstrating a healthy and wealthy personal life as well as commercial success and accolades?

Make a little note here if you do....

_____

_____

_____

_____

CHAPTER 1

Speaking of people those who walk the talk:

What do Elon Musk, Mark Zuckerberg, Barack Obama and Richard Branson have in common. They run their body like their businesses. Each of these leaders, whether you identify with their messages or not, place a very high value on health, wellbeing, family and time to be mentally and physically agile.

They are a great example of being a Fitpreneur of Ultimate Leadership.

For example Mark Zuckerberg is known for sharing his top tips on staying healthy while running a global business[2]

- Choose a goal
- Get your pet involved
- Be Disciplined
- Eat Real Food
- Change your routine
- Give back—make it a charity event or goal within to support a fitness event in the community

Other CEO's claim their personal wellbeing mantra and discipline keeps them mentally sharp and agile as well...

"I've exercised—whether it be lifting or running—religiously for the past 12 years of my life, and it has played a critical role in my daily attitude, work potential, and outlook on life."

Hannibal Baldwin, co-founder and CEO at SiteZeus

"Yoga has helped in so many areas of my life. It forces me to unplug from whatever issue I'm dealing with, spend time as a student, and focus on being present in the moment. I can walk into a studio anywhere in the world and get centered in no time. Early in my career, I would have rolled my eyes reading some executive profess how being on a yoga mat makes them good at business. But I have found a regular practice makes me a better leader, more patient parent, and keeps me sharp mentally and physically."

John Swanciger, CEO of Manta

CHAPTER 1

Finding your Fitpreneur requires that as leader in life, you understand health, wealth and wisdom go hand in hand.

Tenacity, drive and vision are effortless when you have the vitality, sustenance and experience to design the business and the life you love.

Ultimate leadership (or being a Fitpreneur) also means planning financial success for the business and your own legacy. Well rounded leaders understand the need to pay attention to their own finances with integrity as well as the business or organisational bottom line.

The final trifecta is the element of wisdom. Experience cannot be under rated. Learning skills and having years of applying them are two very different things. With time comes wisdom.

It also comes with it the ability to share this wisdom, to make good decisions across all areas of life and to understand yourself as a person and a leader.

We must work on our own self as well as the development of the business.

HEALTHY | WEALTHY | WISE

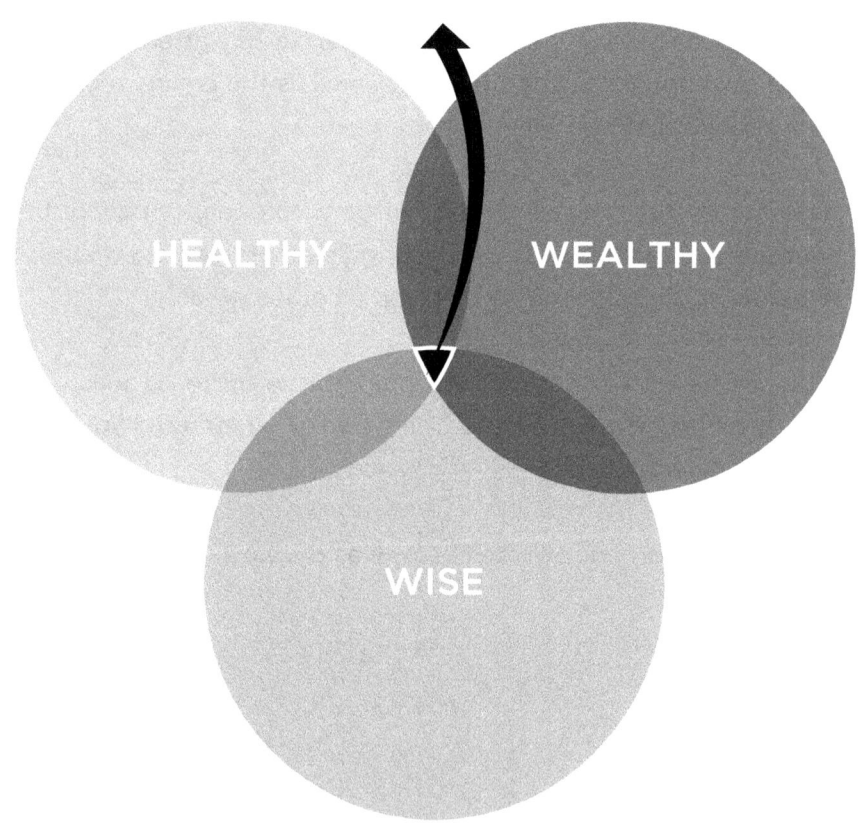

"YOU ARE THE HERO OF YOUR OWN STORY."

NIKKI FOGDEN-MOORE

HEALTHY | WEALTHY | WISE

So What's Stopping You So Far?

Getting a fresh perspective on mindset for leadership.

You'd think we'd have the perfect blend by now, with "time-saving" digital access, flexible working opportunities, a myriad of tips and tools on the world wide web and more awareness about stress and personal development than ever before.

Think again.

More stress, less time, more responsibility, less support. Overall, statistics show lower levels of personal wellbeing and workplace wellbeing, higher levels of stress and depression, and increased anxiety symptoms than ever before.

The top five causes of stress in Australia are[3]:

1. Personal finances – 49 per cent
2. Family issues – 45 per cent
3. Personal health – 44 per cent
4. Trying to maintain a healthy lifestyle – 40 per cent
5. Issues with the health of others close to us – 38 per cent

CBS News America says that personal finances were the significant cause of stress today—with over 64% of executives reporting this as a top reason[4].

Most CEO's and business owners I talk to, workshop with or coach are juggling issues in at least four of these areas.

On top of this there are the core business issues that most CEO's and Fortune 500 Companies and small business owners are facing going into 2016[5]

1. Hiring new employees
2. Increasing profits
3. Providing healthcare to employees
4. Growing revenues
5. Managing cash flow
6. Staying energised
7. Avoiding client dependence

Many leaders fall into the same routine of trying to climb their way out of stress and exhaustion on weekends or holidays, only to find themselves falling back into the same trap when they return to work.

They come to dread the start of a new week and a new load of responsibilities, with seemingly no way out.

Good news is you picked up this book and I'm hopefully going to help you change that direction.

First up let's look at where your Vitality Bank Balance sits with this next chapter....

CHAPTER 2
CHECKS AND BALANCES:
WHERE DO YOU SIT

CHAPTER 2

Before we get started let's do a short exercise that looks at the deposits and long term sustainable success you are creating, versus the withdrawals—the day to day decisions, activities and elements that have you mortgaging the harmony in life as a leader.

Complete a list of elements on the left hand column that you believe add value to your life. Use some of the examples on the following page or add your own. What ever sits in this column must:

- Add energy
- Be a positive impact on finances
- Show awareness for yourself and others
- Contribute to your personal health and wellbeing
- Show that you lead by example
- Demonstrates good use of time
- Reduces stress and anxiety
- Makes you feel great, look great and act to your best potential.

On the RIGHT hand column we are going to list all the things you may do, consume, not do or work on that detract from building you ultimate vitality. Remember this is business and personal.

- These reduce your energy and increase stress levels
- Detract you from sleep and wellbeing choices
- Put you in financial stress
- Show lack of planning

- Demonstrate fears in decision making
- Overall are considered withdrawals on your health, wealth and wisdom

Examples of deposits

- Eating fresh food
- Good nights sleep
- Financial planning
- Completing personal admin weekly or fortnightly
- Good legacy and planning wiht business
- Time out for self and family
- Exercise and fitness regimes
- Medical check ups and considerations
- Holiday and Vacation time
- Creativity and Planning time
- Growth and succession planning
- Time with mentors, advisory committee or trusted sources

Examples of withdrawals

- Lack of sleep
- No breaks in work day
- Behind on finances and personal tax
- No future planning or investment strategy updates
- Stress at work and not coping
- Wrong people in the roles
- High anxiety projects or people
- Lack of time with family and friends
- No ME time or space for creativity and decision making
- Bad deals, tricky finances and issues at work not being resolved
- Lack of support/trusted sources
- No holidays/vacation time out

FILL IN YOUR VITALITY BANK™ BALANCE HERE

Each element scores 5 points
Add up each column
Subtract the withdrawals from the deposits to get your
Vitality Bank™ Balance

DEPOSITS List all the elements in your life that **add value** to your health & wellbeing:	WITHDRAWAL List all the elements in your life that **detract value** to your health & wellbeing:
_____	_____
_____	_____
_____	_____
_____	_____
_____	_____
_____	_____
_____	_____
_____	_____
_____	_____
_____	_____
_____	_____
_____	_____
_____	_____
_____	_____
Sub Total: _____	Sub Total: _____

DEPOSITS less WITHDRAWALS - my Vitality Bank™
Balance is_____

"SOMETIMES THE BIGGEST BARRIERS WE HAVE IN LIFE ARE PURELY OURSELVES... ARE YOU STANDING IN YOUR OWN WAY?"

NIKKI FOGDEN-MOORE

Breaking The Cycle

When business gets tough, maintaining a sense of entrepreneurialism is a challenge.

How do you keep at the front of the pack, make great decisions and stay in top shape for business and personal vitality?

First up, stop and recognise that it takes more than meetings, long lunches and late-night phone calls and hours on the computer. You don't catch up by filling every moment trying to get through the emails, attend all meetings, return all phone calls and not put a sustainable strategy in place.

Skipping more family and friends time or health and fitness for work is not the smart choice in the long term.

Bringing Balance Back

Ultimate leadership takes a presence that exudes longevity, agility, strength of character, intelligence and physical fortitude—whether you're a small start up, an at home mumprenuer or at director level—it's crucial to to create value for yourself and your business in the long term.

As business owners, leaders in life and anyone in corporate knows—the best results are the result of a clear strategy and the courage to make a plan that's relevant, realistic and result driven.

Self Talk(ing you out of things)

Who is that stranger that constantly mutters away in your head. That tells you outlaid what you can already see quite clearly for yourself.

It's an important distinction to take note of your "self-talk" versus YOUR own intuition.

Do you say things to yourself such as, "I can't cope", "I'm too busy", "I'm so tired", "It's not fair", "I can't make this work", or "Why am I doing this?"

Mindset and Mojo

It's no surprise highly driven CEOs complain of feeling stressed and stuck in a rut. Yet, as positivity scholar Barbara Fredrickson states, positivity has a knock-on effect that can help you flourish in all areas of life.

If that's the case, why is it so difficult to turn mental stress around and have a positive mindset?

You may be the one standing in your own way.

More often than not, the biggest barrier to our success is ourselves.

Our old mindset, stories and assumptions hold us back from harmony in business, leadership and life. This is the result of years of feeling you need to prove, strive, perform and deliver.

- Of coming into work first and leaving last.
- Of having long meetings to show your value.
- Of wining and dining as it's the way it's always been done.
- Of coming home late and being too tired to spend quality time with your family "because you need to work this hard to provide a future".
- Not asking for help or bringing in a new style of leadership because "it won't work, we've tried before …"

Well this is all just internal chatter that is not supporting your real performance and impact you can create. In fact it's holding you back.

"75% OF CONVERSATIONS ARE IN OUR HEADS."

NIKKI FOGDEN-MOORE

A Fresh Perspective

If you're fed up with negotiating with yourself more than others, chances are that old stories are holding you back from operating with clarity and conviction. Here are my three vital steps to help you go from chaos to calm and get your mindset mojo back:

- What is really the issue?
- Do you have the information to make an informed decision?
- Is what you are thinking REALLY true?

If you are constantly lying awake at night, getting up in the morning with a feeling of dread and pressure or constantly grappling with doubt, fear and concern then it's time for a mental re-boot.

In the words of speaker and author Byron Katie, do the work.

Ask yourself:

- What is the roadblock, or is it an opportunity?
- Where is the room for growth—emotional, personal and financial—for you and the business?

Strip back the stressful situation to the bare basics of facts and stats. Take out the emotional stories. Be sincere, but be clear.

HEALTHY | WEALTHY | WISE

Getting Back in The Drivers Seat

Step One:
Recognise you that your health is your wealth. Clear decision making happens when we are not stressed and can think without exhaustion and panic. You need to run your body like your business.

Step Two:
Understand that financial planning is for you as well as your business. Are you creating fantastic budgets and growth for the company and at the same time ignoring your own legacy and long term wealth building. Do you feel you are constantly borrowing and leveraging on the future with no real financial foundation right now.

It's time to dive into your personal finances as well as the business to ensure you have a clear idea of where you sit and make a plan for long term prosperity and financial freedom

Step Three:
We don't go through life we GROW through life. A fresh perspective is crucial for ultimate leadership. All too often people feel governed by the circumstances of building and running a business, organisations or having responsibilities as part of a board of directors.

The basic fact is business is always going to require planning, decision making, fire fighting, people and resource issues and market instability.

Don't act so shocked each time. We know this—instead get back in the drivers seat and be regular and religious about planning, know your business and your people landscape. Think ahead.

In the following chapters I am going to give you the tools that will go through each of these steps:

- Recognising where you are now and where you really need to be
- Understanding the tools of running a sustainable business and life—with a wining week and the art of 90-day planning
- Leading others—using your wisdom and experience to demonstrate thoughtful leadership and smart choices. Creating a culture at work and at home that enables ultimate success

And finally we'll touch on the small elements that are so crucial for maintaining this mindset and momentum. A dream team, supporting others and the 90-day adjust and review approach.

What if there was a very simple way to change the pattern of highs and lows, peaks and troughs, and feeling over-worked once and for all?

What if you could learn to blend your business and your personal vitality on a weekly (even daily) basis, without turning your life upside down?

More importantly, what if there was a way you could lead your family and your teams by example for lasting results?

There is and you can.

The next chapter is dedicated to reigniting clarity, running a winning week every week and helping you be a true Fitpreneur.

At the back of this book I've listed some of the podcasts and resources on my blog about breaking negative thoughts and being back in control or finding your focus.

These feature the wonderful Layne Beachley, thoughts guru Trevor Hendy and former CEO Mike Duff all talking about mindset and the power we have to change our thoughts as leaders. Just check out the resources section.

"THERE IS NOTHING MORE POWERFUL THAN WHEN YOUR GOALS AND YOUR ACTIONS ARE TRULY ALIGNED WITH YOUR VALUES AND BELIEFS."

NIKKI FOGDEN-MOORE

CHAPTER 3
WHAT DO YOU VALUE THE MOST

CHAPTER 3

The issue is many of us have not taken time to review goals that are deeper than surface achievements. What if the core of what drives you has changed from when you first kick started your business or career.

- What do you value the most?
- What drives you now?
- What holds you back?

This section is dedicated to helping you check in with your deeper drive and values. It's the inner compass. Your master mindset that when you truly understand what you value the most, it will unlock much more potential in how you lead and succeed in business and in life.

Why bother?

The problem is, many people are not even aware of what's important to them anymore. Are you living by old rules or goals? What worked for you in your 20's most likely does not fit the busy life you have now.

You will have experienced more, learned more about yourself as a person in all areas of life. Yet most high achievers in business I come across have forgotten to take a rewind and review of the next phase—before they hit a massive road block that forces them to do so.

When we are not connected to what we value most then we are governed by the stories we tell ourselves—the should do, the could do etc.

Knowing your values helps you navigate challenges, overcome road blocks and make decisions that will ensure you move forward with authenticity.

As responsibilities, schedules and weekly demands change, so, too, must your approach to health and wellbeing, planning your finances, how you work with people and thinking about creating a legacy.

Can our values change?

Undeniably, our goals and dreams change as we grow through life. There is generally a curve to BE, DO, HAVE and WANT before we think about what we really need and can give back. What motivated you in the past will change as your life moves through different phases.

Your job, title, travel and experiences may have been at the top of your list in your 20s.

Setting up your career and building a name for yourself was probably more important throughout your 30s and 40s.

Perhaps you started a family and the dynamic of why you were working became more about providing than proving.

Are you working yourself so much that you're physically over-stressed and emotionally under-nourished? Do kindness and love feature at the top of your list, or do financial success, recognition and prosperity come first?

- What, in your day, fits with what you value the most?
- When was the last time you deeply thought about this?

Many of you won't find these questions easy to answer. The good news is that when you take a moment to reflect on what values resonate with you, a whole new perspective opens up.

Giving Yourself Permission

Letting go of where you think you should be and taking a moment to define what is deeply important to you can have a life-changing effect on the way you run your life. It can be as simple as replacing hour-long meetings with "walk and talks", encouraging you (and your staff) to leave desks for lunch, and taking a quick break outside for some fresh air.

It can be looking at your week and ensuring you are planning who you hang out with, where you spend your time and what you do with those very few spare minutes. Above all else it's about having a new game plan that is relevant to where you are now and where you want to be going.

It's knowing first and foremost what is TRULY the most important value to you now.

HEALTHY | WEALTHY | WISE

- Why do you do what you do?
- What do you want to get from others?
- Is it respect, financial reward, kindness, happiness or recognition?

From the following list, what top three values speak to you the most?

Don't ask anyone else.

Find a quiet place and feel what resonates. Choose the three most important, nonnegotiable values that take priority over everything else for you.

Important tips:

1. There is ALWAYS an answer. Don't rush through this and do the chemistry check.
2. Listen to your real intuition on this. No one else. Once you have circled your top 3 values—close your eyes, place your hand on your sternum where (the top of your rib cage meet—referred also in yoga or mindfulness as a chakra) and ask yourself out of the 3 circled—which of these is your absolute NON-NEGOTIABLE.
3. The other way to look at it is the value you hold the highest regard and importance for is often the one you feel wronged by the most when others do not demonstrate this value. It can be easier to ask which value absolutely is the most important thing I need and expect from those closest to me. Usually this is the most important and what you expect from yourself.

Step 1: Identify the times when you were happiest

Find examples from both your career and personal life. This will ensure some balance in your answers.

- What were you doing?
- Were you with other people?
- Who?
- What other factors contributed to your happiness?

Step 2: Identify the times when you were most proud

Use examples from your career and personal life.

- Why were you proud?
- Did other people share your pride? Who?
- What other factors contributed to your feelings of pride?

NOTES

CHAPTER 3

CORE VALUES LIST

Authenticity	Achievement	Adventure
Authority	Autonomy	Balance
Beauty	Boldness	Compassion
Challenge	Citizenship	Community
Competency	Contribution	Creativity
Curiosity	Determination	Fairness
Faith	Fame	Friendships
Fun	Growth	Happiness
Honesty	Humour	Influence
Inner Harmony	Justice	Kindness
Knowledge	Leadership	Learning
Love	Loyalty	Meaningful Work
Openness	Optimism	Peace
Pleasure	Poise	Popularity
Recognition	Religion	Reputation
Respect	Responsibility	Security
Self-Respect	Service	Spirituality
Stability	Success	Status
Trustworthiness	Wealth	Wisdom

NOTES

WRITE DOWN YOUR 3 MOST IMPORTANT VALUES

_____
_____
_____
_____
_____
_____
_____
_____
_____

IDENTIFY YOUR NON-NEGOTIABLE VALUE

_____
_____
_____
_____
_____
_____
_____
_____
_____

Check your top-priority values, and make sure they fit with your life and your vision for yourself.

Do these values make you feel good about yourself?

- Are you proud of your top three values?
- Would you be comfortable and proud to tell your values to people you respect and admire?
- Do these values represent things you would support, even if your choice isn't popular, and it puts you in the minority?

When you consider your values in decision making, you can be sure to keep your sense of integrity and what you know is right, and approach decisions with confidence and clarity. You'll also know that what you're doing is best for your current and future happiness and satisfaction.

Making value-based choices may not always be easy. However, making a choice that you know is right is a lot less difficult in the long run.

Do you think your values have changed from 10 years ago? Perhaps you'll be surprised that they have been the same all along.

"GOOD SKILLS
CAN BE LEARNT
BUT GREAT VALUES
COME FROM
WITHIN."

NIKKI FOGDEN-MOORE

HEALTHY | WEALTHY | WISE

Being Real

Don't be afraid to be honest. This is your life. The more you step into who you truly are, the more you will enjoy life and succeed in life.

Identifying what truly makes you tick can unleash a whole new momentum in the way you communicate to others, understand your leadership/parenting style, acknowledge ways to set and reward goals, and help those close to you give you what you need.

If you're a manager, consider what motivates the people you manage deep down. It may not be a pay rise or fancy corner office—it may actually be more time with their family, whom they value above cash and long hours.

If you're going for a new role or promotion, think about what you feel most connected with. How can you communicate to your team and management what motivates you?

Values are the things that you believe are important in the way you live and work.

If you liked this exercise, why not share it with your friends and family?

Take a moment in your team meeting and get to know the people you work with. What truly motivates them?

How can you give back with understanding? The more we understand ourselves and those around us, the more fulfilling our lives, interactions, work and connections are.

"VALUES ARE LIKE FINGERPRINTS, NOBODY'S ARE THE SAME BUT YOU LEAVE THEM ALL OVER EVERYTHING YOU DO."

ELVIS PRESLEY

CHAPTER 3

NOTES

CHAPTER 4

GOAL SETTING: NOT JUST ANOTHER TO DO LIST

"THERE ARE
365 DAYS IN A YEAR
SOMEDAY ISN'T
ONE OF THEM."

NIKKI FOGDEN-MOORE

Reality Check

What will it cost you if you do not make a change?

I don't want this to be just another book, just another to do list or one of those elements you feel all fired up about and 6 months later nothing has changed. BLAH! I really dislike inertia and serial consuming without action.

What are you waiting for? This is it. There is literally no time like the present. What has worked for you in the past got you to this point. How do you want to live and lead going forward.

It's time to get off autopilot. This tiny little chapter is just to remind you that you have one life and one body, Fedex is not going to be sending you a new set of both tomorrow.

It's never too late.

Just remember: Cutting back on corporate health, and your own health and wellbeing impacts your culture, connection and performance on all levels. From home to the boardroom.

- What's the point of putting everything into your job/career if you're only to burn out afterwards.
- Are you sabotaging yourself and your business by not paying attention to the every day balance?
- Are you taking shortcuts on how you use time for you, your staff and those around you in terms of quality of life, health, family time, space for creativity and social activities?

Let me be clear for one moment.

Being a Fitpreneur is not about stopping the passion, drive and love for what you do in business. It is ensuring you are absolutely able to enjoy the journey along the way and design a life that ensures you can handle the demands, pressures and high energy required to run a sustainable and successful business, make great decisions.

This sounds simple enough and but what's stopping you?

- Too busy
- Responsibilities
- Just have to get this project finished
- I'll take a break on holidays
- I can't afford to take time out
- I have to do it all myself
- I need to answer this now

Most probably it's your mindset—The next chapter is how to build a winning week, goals that really count and bring it all together. Let's go!

Write all that stuff down now here:

WHAT HAVE YOU TRIED BEFORE THAT NEVER WORKED?

_____

_____

_____

_____

_____

_____

_____

WHAT LISTS DO YOU MAKE THAT NEVER HAPPEN?

_____

_____

_____

_____

_____

_____

_____

_____

"LEARN TO INTEGRATE, NOT NEGOTIATE YOUR TIME."

NIKKI FOGDEN-MOORE

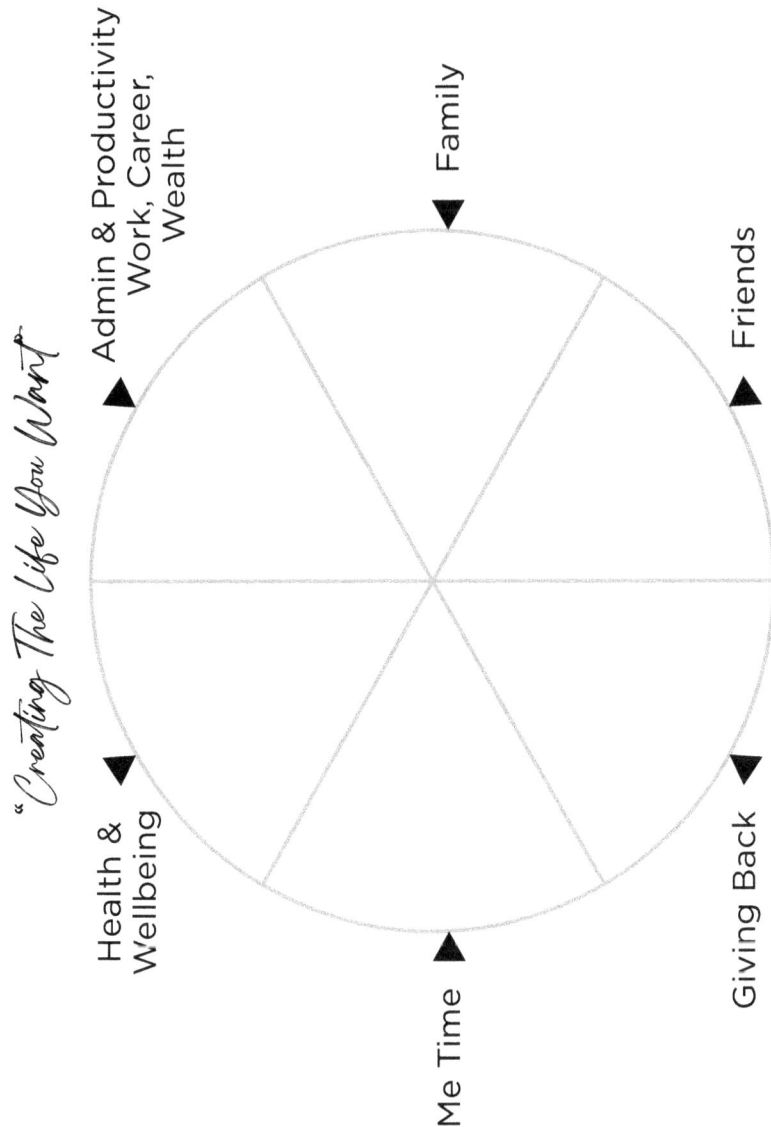

HEALTHY | WEALTHY | WISE

You: Healthy, Wealthy and Wise

Have a quick glance at the 6 Pillars Of Vitality and take a few minutes to fill in the sections with the most colour representing the pillar you spend the most of your time in.

Where do you sit right now on balancing your business and your personal success?

For example if you spend most of your time at work and with your family then you will colour in those sections as much as you feel—80% admin/productivity and 20% of your time family. Sounds drastic but be honest and take time to think about it.

Once you've done that consider the gaps.

WRITE DOWN HERE THE AREAS YOU SPEND MOST OF YOUR TIME (IF IT'S ONLY 2 PILLARS THEN JUST WRITE 2)

_____

_____

_____

_____

_____

_____

_____

_____

WRITE DOWN HERE THE AREAS YOU SPEND THE LEAST OF YOUR TIME

_____
_____
_____
_____
_____
_____
_____
_____

WHERE COULD YOU PUT MORE FOCUS

_____
_____
_____
_____
_____
_____
_____
_____
_____
_____

NOTES

NOTES

CHAPTER 5
BRINGING IT ALL TOGETHER

"A GOAL IS A DREAM SET TO PAPER DON'T JUST THINK IT INK IT."

NIKKI FOGDEN-MOORE

CHAPTER 5

Leading From Within

Where do people struggle the most when it comes to achieving their dreams? I'd say in these three key areas:

1. Conviction for their goal.
2. Consistency of action and dedicating time to it.
3. Communicating to others that they need support.

A true Fitpreneur knows the importance of cultivating business and personal vitality to achieve lasting results.

All aspects of your life need to be seamlessly integrated, not compartmentalised.

Look back to the 6 Pillars Of Ultimate Vitality wheel. You must be prepared to think differently about the way you balance work, home life, friends, family, "me" time and wellbeing. In this next chapter, I will show you how.

First Up The Power of The 90-Day Plan

The 90-day plan is not a new concept—in fact, it's used in almost all the coaching, business and development plans I know, and it works.

When's the last time you actually made a 90-day plan that looked at EVERY part of your life. Not just budgets?

- Are you on auto pilot or are you living a life you love? (truly)
- Are you working with people who inspire you?
- Are you connected to friends who support you?
- Do you share a life with those you feel you can be yourself with?

In today's environment, it's a real challenge to set personal goals. There is so much out there, especially on social media, to compare ourselves to. I call it "generation exhibition".

We have lost connection with what's real. Mantras and meditations do not work unless your goal is truly aligned with your inner why. Set goals and dreams that are yours. Create authentic plans and visions that connect.

It all starts with making sure your goal is relevant to you, not someone else.

CHAPTER 5

Do you have lots of great ideas, wish lists, mood boards and to-dos that never eventuate to anything? Is procrastination and day-to-day life getting in the way of creating the life you would love?

Ever wondered what everyone is going on about with their 90-day plans?

Do you think it's just for your business? Think again.

Know your personal goals as well as your business goals, and ensure these 2 pillars they are blended within a winning week blend together.

Start with your 90-day plan, and work back from there. Remember it's not just about the finances and business it's also building in your personal development, wellbeing and enjoyment in life too.

The basic element of designing the life you want and actually sustaining a Fitpreneur approach is being able to adjust and review every 90 days.

Think of it as adjusting the sails in a boat as you may need to go the safest or fastest route to your destination.

The practical art of planning in 360 degrees is a powerful one.

A simple, effective tool to ensure that you stay focused and on point with your goals.

- Talk less about your resolutions "I am going to do.." and more about creating action "my tasks this week are…"
- Work on your focus for what you want to achieve by the end of 90 days = goals
- Determine how you're going to get there in 90-day = actions
- Detail 3 immediate things you can do straight away to get the ball rolling = tasks
- Understand the driving force behind your conviction and purpose.
- Make sure the goals you write down are relevant to you and resonate

I recommend you do this exercise every 90 days and find someone you can have as an accountability partner or a master mind group with whom you can share all there areas—healthy, wealthy and wise elements you are working on.

6 Key steps to develop your 90-day plan:

1. Download and print the 90-day worksheet from my 90-Day Plan podcast post https://www.nikkifogdenmoore.com/podcasts/radical-self-belief-the-mojo-maker-podcast/episodes/2147556197.
2. Choose what THREE goals you would like to achieve in the next 90 days.
3. Write where you need to be, or what actions need to happen in 30 days to be on track to accomplish your quarterly goals.
4. Determine what specific tasks you can do in the next seven days to build momentum.
5. Write down negative thoughts that are preventing you from achieving your goals. (THE EXCUSES LIST)
6. Pick THREE things you can do TODAY to set yourself up to reach your 90-day goal. Right now.[6]

HEALTHY | WEALTHY | WISE

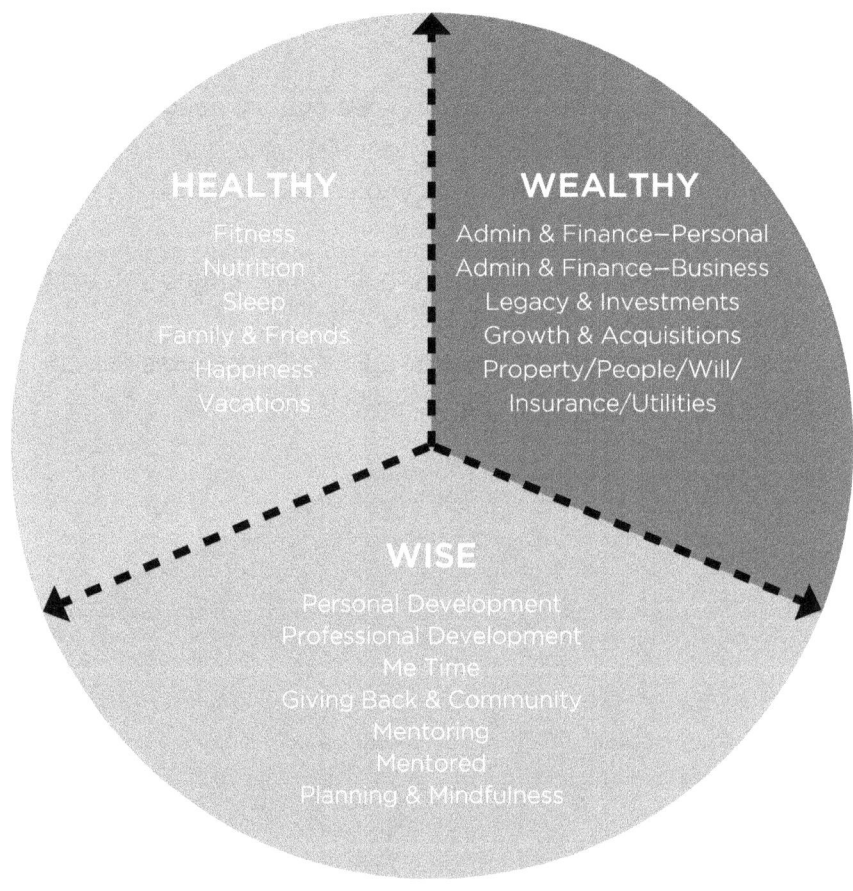

"A SENSE OF PURPOSE IS A PRIVILEGE."

BILLIE JEAN KING

HEALTHY | WEALTHY | WISE

Know Your Why—This is Essential To Success

What is the reason behind your goal?

What do you really, deeply want as the outcome?

When you have a true connection with and conviction for your goal (no matter how big or small that goal is), you never need to over explain, negotiate with yourself or convince others. It's your beacon, your true north, and it keeps you going.

Trouble Shooting - no goal - no worries.

- What if you don't know what you want?
- What if you have NO clue what makes you happy?
- What if you're fine with the right now, just as it is?

If you haven't yet taken the time to consider what's next, and you're suddenly asked what you want, by when and how are you going to get there, it can create enormous pressure.

Be inspired by what others achieve, but define goals that are relevant and unique to you. Find your WHY.

When you have a strong conviction, you won't go off track.

- Ask yourself, "Are these my goals?
- Are they important to me?
- Would I do anything possible to achieve them?"

If you can answer yes, you're right on track.

If you don't have your 90-day plan done yet, don't panic.

What if someone close to you or in your team isn't motivated like you?

Don't judge. If you're one of those souls fired up with purpose and passion, that's fantastic. I know how you feel. I've been fortunate enough to have had a strong inner compass for more than a decade. It has kept me on track to create vitality in all that I do. Lucky us!

However, I want to give you a gentle reminder that our role as Fitpreneurs is to understand that others have a different path. You need to accept that. You can't bully others into having a goal right now.

When we have passion, purpose and clarity, it's a privilege. It's not easy to come by. Some people may never figure out what their direction in life is, as it's the journey that makes up their road map.

Let go of any judgement. Be there to support, share ideas and encourage whenever possible—but only if asked.

HEALTHY | WEALTHY | WISE

NOTES

"IF YOU DON'T DESIGN
WHAT YOU WANT
YOU'LL GET WHAT
YOU'RE GIVEN."

NIKKI FOGDEN-MOORE

HEALTHY | WEALTHY | WISE

Bringing it All Together, the BLEND

Great leadership is understanding the importance of combining personal accountability with commercial responsibility. Fitpreneurs are dedicated to maintaining their health and wellbeing, while at the same time intelligently and efficiently running their business.

As a Fitpreneur it's about planning your week every week with purpose and intent.

On a side note I read that quote when I was 12 and never forgotten it.

You must continually integrate into your daily life the five key pillars of performance:

I. Health and fitness
II. Admin
III. Productivity
IV. Friends/family
V. ME time
VI. Giving Back

"PLAN YOUR WINNING WEEK. CREATE YOUR WINNING MONTH. ENJOY YOUR WINNING YEAR."

NIKKI FOGDEN-MOORE

HEALTHY | WEALTHY | WISE

Plan a Winning Week—Every Week

You've probably looked up lately and realised you have been last on your to-do list. You've never quite been able to give your own health and vitality the same focus as your commercial endeavours.

It's that tiny gap—you can see it, you know it—but for some reason achieving regular balance, mindfulness and a healthy lifestyle is a gap that you can't quite fill.

Clear thinking, a sense of calm and the ability to manage stressful situations are vital to strong in leadership whether at home, for yourself, your family and for your business.

Being successful financially and having accolades at work should not come at the cost of your personal health and wellbeing.

"MY MOTTO:
YOU NEED TO RUN
YOUR BODY
LIKE YOU DO
YOUR BUSINESS."

NIKKI FOGDEN MOORE

HEALTHY | WEALTHY | WISE

Here's How To Plan Your Winning Week Effectively

STEP 1. Make a Planning Session Every Sunday

This weekly routine will set you up for the week ahead. It will help you plan with your spouse and family to ensure that all the important elements in life are covered. This is your chance to be in control and define how you want your week to run.

STEP 2. Write Out Your Week

Use a big sheet of paper or weekly planning overview (download the simple worksheet for weekly planning from the links in the resource section of the book) and in the left-hand corner, bullet point the following five elements:

- **FITNESS & WELLBEING.** By scheduling wellness and fitness first, you ensure they are a priority. Exercise boosts brainpower, reduces stress and can increase productivity in the workplace. This should be part of your strategy for peak performance and work-life balance.
- **ADMIN/WORK PRODUCTIVITY.** Aside from day-to-day meetings and work load, keep your personal finances, vision board, ideas and weekly planning up to date. Write an overview of your tasks for the week and set Monday morning or mid-week update sessions with yourself to review what you need to take care of. Being in control of your life also means planning finances, administration and higher education. Don't leave it to the last minute—schedule at least 14 minutes a week for this. This will be 1% of your day well spent.

- **FRIENDS.** Book at least one catch up during the week with someone you love hanging out with. Better still, combine it with something healthy and active, or discover a new restaurant renowned for delicious, healthy food.
- **FAMILY.** Schedule quality family time, even if it's a phone call or Skype chat with loved ones overseas. Try to do something fun and active with your immediate family.
- **ME TIME.** Ah! The one aspect so many people let go of when their schedule fills up. If you do not value time for yourself, how can you expect others to value your time? Dedicate 14 minutes of your day to yourself. You need down time to think, breathe and calibrate. It allows your intuition to answer the burning questions without distraction or interruption.
- **GIVING BACK.** The 6th Pillar—it can be on a small scale at home, work, mentoring, just doing random acts of kindness or spending more time with your family without distractions. Charity starts at home but it goes way beyond.

STEP 3. Making it Live

Transfer your written week to your digital agenda.

Update your PA, team and any necessary "stakeholders" on time that is unavailable for bookings. By setting boundaries, you provide people with the opportunity to work effectively with you. Leading a team starts with leading yourself.

Set a great example. If you're at home and running a busy household, then put your agenda on the fridge so your family can see what you've got planned.

STEP 4. Be Consistent

Do all of this weekly! Weekly work creates monthly change and helps you fasttrack your goals. Ultimately, you need to design your ideal life, rather than wait for someone else to do it for you. Make it happen.

STEP 5: Be Smart

Running a business and balancing home/personal life is exhausting, so bring harmony and wellbeing into focus.

Don't throw yourself into hard-core training, new career development and strict regimes you cannot sustain.

Be flexible by allowing space for life. Things will pop up and you'll need to have some degree of flexibility, but the foundation of your week should be established well before Monday morning.

I am right behind the philosophy of planning and, more importantly, executing. In fact, it's a cornerstone of my Vitality Road MapTM and crucial for you to create the life you want. However, I believe even more so that you need to take time to ensure the goals and actions you set are relevant, resonate and are "real time".

Check in with the 3 R's of each time you design your winning week.

THE WINNING WEEK WORKSHEET

1. Healthy & Wellbeing
Health, fitness, nutrition, meal planning, programs adn day to day wellness etc.

4. Admin & Productivity
Work goals, project bills, budgets, strategy, learning and education

2, 3. Friends & Family
Who do you want to hang out with this week, family commitments, social

5. ME Time
Time alone, doing the things you love, reflection, quiet and relaxation.

THE 5 ELEMENTS OF MY WINNING WEEK

NOTES

My 3 R's of Goal Setting Each Week

RELEVANT: Is this relevant to you and your overall mission? Is it relevant to your business and what you want for your family? Or were you just inspired by someone else's life on Instagram? What is VITAL that you do this week?

RESONATE: Your goal overall and how it plays out this week… Is this truly something that is meaningful to you? Is it a goal you stand behind?

REAL TIME: Can you make milestones on a daily and weekly basis to boost your progress? What are those—make them tangible. This is a must achieve not a nice to have list.

Keep it simple.

"IF YOU AIM AT NOTHING YOU WILL HIT IT EVERY TIME."

B.J. MARSHALL

NOTES

CHAPTER 6
LEADING OTHERS

"GREAT LEADERS DON'T TELL YOU WHAT TO DO, THEY SHOW YOU HOW IT'S DONE."

NIKKI FOGDEN-MOORE

CHAPTER 6

In my experience working with CEOs and entrepreneurs over the past 15+ years, no matter what size the business, these three pillars of leadership build trust, create unity and empower others.

It's not just a matter of having vision and giving direction, it's showing an authentic connection to the why and engaging teams at all levels along the way.

Running a business is not just about focusing on the numbers; it is about keeping the value in your staff, your vision and the momentum in good times and bad.

When we truly lead from within and lead by example, we have a clear platform togenuinely lead others.

We are able to build trust and credibility. I like to call it earning your stripes. People will follow leaders who truly believe in the principles and best practice they hand down.

Ask yourself, what it will take to roll out the new culture or process?

Have you tried and tested the roadmap with your senior team and know the "why" with clarity and conviction?

Plan your roll out and the buy-in. Having a plan on how you are going to lead others helps make change, growth and development as seamless as possible.

Stay connected to this initiative and monitoring its progress. Get feedback and navigate roadblocks efficiently. Empower others to implement the changes required.

A crucial element of being a manager or leader is recognising that your actions speak louder than words.

When we practice what we preach and share experiences with others in ways they find relevant and applicable, the results can be amazing. Think of the leaders you admire. They have the natural ability to be visionary, demonstrate their conviction and inspire others to follow.

Know your strengths, identify productive alliances and show open communication with your management and executive team.

With your direct reports, share your why, show the journey and practice what you preach.

THE FITPRENEUR 3 PILLARS OF LEADERSHIP

"LEAD FROM WITHIN. LEAD BY EXAMPLE. AND ONLY THEN YOU CAN LEAD OTHERS AUTHENTICALLY."

NIKKI FOGDEN-MOORE

Lead By Example Before You Can Lead Others

The largest asset an organisation has is its people. The organisational culture we create does not come from words on paper but the actions of those in charge. Ask yourself—do you know your staff?

Do you genuinely connect with them, or are you always too busy and stressed? What messages do you give them with your presentation and behaviour?

Here are three ways to fast track that right now:

Look Up

Got your head so buried in paperwork you're missing what's right in front of you? Great CEOs are connected to their business landscape. They feel the minor tremors when things are off track. They spot the small signs before a bigger disaster hits.

Where there's smoke, there's fire. What's going on inside the business and how are your customers responding? Get your direct reports together and do a quick health check of operations.

- Are people paying attention to detail on budgets and acquisitions?
- Are products being delivered as per the quality and values of the business?
- Are volume-based KPIs creating a "shortcut" mentality, where more mistakes can happen?
- Are staff over worked, detached and exhausted? Do they miss details and fail to adhere to health and safety rules?
- Are there more incident reports than before?

Look Out

Most industries have been around long enough that there are stats and facts on the peaks and troughs of the business. The seven-year cycle for oil and gas, the early adopter to market saturation for tech, the international trends for finance and retail… If you're feeling overwhelmed by day-to-day operations, it is time for you to become better engaged with the trends and where your organisation is positioned within the cycle.

Look back at your experience. Draw on your history and engage your board to think with a helicopter perspective of where the business and its challenges sit on your organisational timeline. Should you be sweating the small stuff, or should you be looking for unorthodox yet real teamwork to get you through?

Look Within

Get back to basics. Why did you want to be a leader in the first place? What attracted you to the role of CEO/Business Owner/Entrepeneur?

Be honest—it's different for everyone. It could be the accolades, the financial reward, the thrill of making a real difference—or just the ability to steer your own ship and work from home!

More often than not, leaders lose their momentum when overwhelmed with board and stakeholder requirements, lack of flexibility to deploy vision and inspiration within the organisation, and a feeling of isolation (as a leader, you don't want to reveal your vulnerability—where in fact this is a crucial element being able to ask for help and learn out loud).

The Australian Workplace Wellness survey[7] stated that the challenge for employers is to take a strategic, measurable approach to human capital.

This starts with you as a leader. Show your team that you treat your health like your wealth. It will encourage them to find their sense of purpose, in and out of office hours.

Also, identify the people inside your organisation who demonstrate clear-headed personal accountability.

Tap into them, make them part of your dream team, and set them as an example for others to follow. Strength in numbers and it creates a great ripple effect.

It's not just about you it's the culture you create at home and at work.

NOTES

CHAPTER 7
THE ADJUST AND REVIEW

Gold Stars For Adults

Why do we stop rewarding milestones along the way?

Part of creating the life you want is being able to identify goals and strategise how to achieve them. The problem is that most of us get so caught up in setting goals, we forget to enjoy the journey and acknowledge the small wins along the way.

- Employees don't trust that genuine support is there to stay. It usually kicks off with a bang, but after six months, no one is there to champion the cause.
- More people turn up for work but don't actually do anything—the "show-up" mentality.
- Financial and leadership decisions become blurred as people are stressed, overworked and overwhelmed.
- Without a culture of transparency, people hide their exhaustion, lack of knowledge and concerns about change. They do not step up with initiative.

The adjust and review is a critical part of being an ultimate leader and FITPERNEUR.

It allows you to assess where you have com in the last 90 days, review your plans and strategise the next 90 days with focus and conviction. Celebrate small wins too.

Reminder. If you don't DO the work—it won't work!

Seriously sometimes I wonder that when people read a book, go to a seminar or a conference you think they expect fairy dust and it just all gets figured out. News flash.

This is actually up to you to make your ultimate life and business happen.

Gold stars for adults works just as well at home as it does at work. Share your monthly and weekly goals with the core people around you and get your colleagues or your family to reward you when they see you demonstrate actions or complete tasks that part of your plan and commitment.

I designed the **Gold Stars for Adults** worksheets for companies I was working with to start making the BLEND of personal and business goals more transparent. We also suggested they take it home and create one where the whole family could get involved.

Head to the resources section in my book for the downloads and worksheet.

Random Acts Of Kindness—
Giving Back Is Always In-Style

The 6th pillar of Vitality and part of the Wise element of being a Fitpreneur is contribution to others.

Giving back doesn't just have to be about financial philanthropy. It's also about giving back your time, experience and elements in your life that can add value and support for others. Even starting as close to home as spending time and helping your own family and friends.

- Start with you
- Start at Home
- Lead by Example at Work
- Choose Charities that Resonate
- Give Back Within Your Means

To Give Back Really Starts with Yourself

I know this may sound selfish but I mean this in the regard to ensuring you are in your best position to help others.

* Are you being kind to yourself? Are you feeding yourself nutritious healthy food that will help your body operating in the optimum?
* Are you treating yourself to health benefits such as exercise, fitness and activities that you enjoy that are good for your cardiac condition and for your overall well-being?
* Are you giving back with time alone when you can read and regenerate and even just taking a moment out to meditate or whatever it is to make sure you're complete and replete, body, mind and soul? So, first of all, start out personally.

Unless you give back to yourself and create time to nurture for you to actually top up your vitality bank, for you to consider your emotional intelligence, your financial planning, figuring out what's purposeful in your life, planning your winning week and making those moments of giving back also for you.

At Home

The first thing I have to say is if you're going to choose a charity or start thinking "how can I contribute", think about places in the environment you live so you can already start giving back just in your daily moments, so there's number one at home with family and friends.

- Choose cruelty-free and eco-friendly cleaning products,
- Recycle—start living with consciousness and you'll already start giving back on a daily basis.
- Walk outside your front yard "Do I know my neighbours? Can I bake a cake for someone? Is someone ill? Do they need to be dropped at the hospital? Do they need care? Can I pick up the groceries?"
- What can you do for a neighbour or a friend that maybe isn't going to reach out to you, but you can reach out to them and say, "Hey, how can I help?".

Whatever is going to help people in times of need, it could be much closer than you think.

- Don't turn a blind eye to those small at-home moments where you can be giving back.
- Think about being more connected with those closest to you.

- Spend a little more time off the computer and more time with your kids. So why not after dinner turn your iPad off, turn your computer off, and spend time engaging with your children before they go to bed.
- Spend time with your partner.
- "Make it count," even if it's just baking a cake for someone, spending the moment really sitting down the level of your child and reading them a story. Really be at that moment.

At Work

There's industry fulfilment in places that you can give back as a professional as an expert in your field, provide guidance and mentoring and support. Corporate consciousness is key no matter what level you are within an organisation. Giving back just also means doing day-to-day things inside the workplace, the good mentor, as a partner, the colleague, as a team player.

For example, if you've been in a role and someone comes up on board that is new, how can you help that person?

Can you help a charity by doing a fun run or activity that will also act as a team building exercise?

There are endless ways to create change and give back in the workplace? It's really coming with good intentions and making sure that you're contributing to that environment.

Choose a Charity that Resonates

Want to sponsor or donate? First of all, find out the facts.

- Who is this person?
- Who is this charity?
- What is this event?
- How much of the money or the time that you are putting in would be used directly for that cause?

There's always information that's made transparent on websites or you can ask directly. Find out where your investments of time and energy and finances are really going.

- Do your research

Do you know enough about them before you start signing up? Instead of buying an animal from a breeder, could you adopt a pet instead and give them a second chance with a new home? I know from my experience this is extremely rewarding.

Give Within Your Means

Know how much time and or money you can afford to invest before you promise the world:

How much time do you actually have or could you provide towards this before you start to jump in and get off and suddenly tell everyone that creating some moment or you're going to volunteer/donate.

Figure out how much time or money you genuinely can put into it first, so you set clear expectations and you're not starting something you cannot finish. If you're providing finances for a non-profit organisation where you're donating regularly to and they're promising you certain things, follow-up and find out where it is going.

Don't just donate and stop thinking about it.

It will make you feel genuine in regards to your contribution, and others respectful and grateful that you are providing as much as you can.

"IF EVERY AMERICAN DONATED 5 HOURS A WEEK OF THEIR TIME, IT WOULD BE EQUAL TO THE LABOUR OF TWENTY MILLION FULL-TIME VOLUNTEERS."

WHOOPI GOLDBERG

CHAPTER 8

FINDING YOUR DREAM TEAM:
STRENGTH IN NUMBERS

"ONE OF THE BEST MOVES IS TO SURROUND YOURSELF WITH FRIENDS WHO INSTEAD OF ASKING 'WHY' ARE QUICK TO SAY 'WHY NOT'."

OPRAH WINFREY

CHAPTER 8

Finding (Or Designing) Your Dream Team

Whether you're a CEO, senior manager or a budding entrepreneur—it's not your office walls, the plaque outside or the stationery bearing your logo that matters.

It's the people factor.

Who is in your corner. Who do you trust, admire and who supports you the most.

You may recall a moment in time when you voiced a new goal—whether it was starting the business, getting back into shape, running a half marathon, going to the gym, taking some time out or quitting sugar!

Once you had bravely put this out there you notice that people might test your conviction, lead you astray, challenge the fact you can do it—or even just not support you at all?!

It's human nature for many people to challenge others goals when they wish they could get up and do something themselves. It can be really confronting for people to see you step up and put your goals into action.

It will also show you the people who genuinely want you to be happy too!

Family and Friends

You may find that the ones you love the most are the least supportive. Well don't take this personally.

As the saying goes it tells you more about them that you—so you need a fast and genuine strategy for support and encouragement for at home and your wider circle.

Ultimately do not give up and don't get discouraged. This is an important lesson to engage in your own journey, your own goals and take control for yourself.

At Work

Running a company or starting one, can be a lonely road—paved with mistakes and minefields that many before you have walked before. It is very rare that what you're going through when building your empire and your legacy, has not in some way been encountered, overcome and traversed by others in your field or just in business and in life.

Cue thinking about expert advice and your dream team—not just in the board room at a governance level but a real group of hand selected people who you know, like and trust to have your absolute best interests at heart.

CHAPTER 8

From personal to commercial finance, recruitment/people and hr to planning your personal wellbeing and mental fortitude.

A dream team is comprised of those who can assist you in all areas of being the best version of yourself—as a person and as a leader. They should cover all areas of your business and life—health, wealth and wisdom.

This is not a new concept but what approach should you take when you are recruiting your pit crew and it's not just about business?

Building Your Team

Quite simply put it, once you embark on a goal of being your personal best in what ever you do, it's crucial to have the right people around you who will encourage, support and be excited for you as you go through each milestone.

Your dream team can be made up of family, of friends, a mentor, your trainer/coaches, your work colleagues, people your workout with, a wellness community online or those you get advice from.

However they must be those who want to see you succeed, and those that have the qualities listed below. Your dream team can even include your kids as you engage them in your goals and show them how much their support means to you.

Your dream team are people who are truly:

1. Authentic in what they do (practice what they preach and are happy for your successes too)
2. Knowledgable (if they are in a coaching/trainer role for you)
3. Positive—about themselves and you as well
4. Genuinely interested in your achievements, milestones, trials and tribulations. If you are hiring a personal trainer he/she MUST be vested in your success, tailoring your program and supporting you along the way. This is not about how good they look in the mirror but you are a reflection of their knowledge, professionalism and what they do!

As you venture into a Fitpreneur lifestyle there may be some 'support casualties' along the way of some friends, family members or colleagues that are not a part of your mentality to work hard on what you love and who you are.

Keep an eye on what is important to you and the long-term benefits of wellness, wealth and wisdom, versus the short-term gratification of fitting in.

Surrounding yourselves with others that share a similar journey, outlook and approach can make the world of difference.

How can you get those you love on board?

Firstly communicate about your goals and be clear about how important this is for you.

Empower your family by asking them for their love, help and support.

- Make a fun schedule you can put on the fridge for your kids to give YOU stars when you achieve your goals each day— even if one of those is to be home a little bit earlier in time to read a story.
- Include them in your fitness and healthy eating or lifestyle elements that show balance and consistency. Do as much as you can together. Cook together, go outside on the weekends or in the afternoon and be active together, discover a new sport you can do as a family like biking, stand up paddling, hiking or just long walks with the dog.

Lead by example—if you are making positive changes be rest assured you are setting a great example for your children on how to look after their health, wealth and being great leaders too.

NOTES

NOTES

CHAPTER 9

ENJOY THE JOURNEY

"BECAUSE OF ROUTINE
WE FORGET THAT
LIFE IS A SERIES OF
ONGOING ADVENTURES."

MAYA ANGELOU

Enjoying the Journey

So you're well on your way to leading as a Fitpreneur.

You've defined your most important values, you're planning your winning week, established your 90-day goals and then, low and behold, life gets in the way.

Fact: Things in business and in life are GOING to be out of your control.

It's not what happens to us it's how we deal with things that counts.

The more we strive, the more we take on responsibilities and this requires more decisions, balance and constant consideration.

MY ULTIMATE MANTRA FOR LEADERS

"THINK LIKE A CEO PLAN LIKE A VISIONARY ACT LIKE A BUDDHA"

NIKKI FOGDEN-MOORE

CHAPTER 9

How To Deal With Times Of Stress

It's going to happen so what's the best way to cope with extremely busy periods during your year or the guaranteed element of the unexpected.

I created this mantra for the leaders I work with. It's an instant reboot for my high achieving, fast-paced clients when they hit roadblocks.

It does not mean you have to be an expert in all areas of business—quite the contrary.

A great leader can recognise the need to delegate. They know the values and skills they need around them. They can step back to evaluate on a daily basis—or even by the minute, depending on the pace of their business and the challenges at hand.

The 3 principles behind this mantra and why it works:

1. **Think like a CEO** (Wearing the commercially strategic hat)— Leadership

Making commercial decisions, hiring new staff, planning marketing campaigns, forming partner alliances and thinking about whether or not to attend a conference all come down to how the use of time, resources and finances impact your bottom line.

When making decisions, ask yourself: What's the return on investment? Does it fit with the overall brand and company strategy? Will this action lead you closer to your business goals?

Approach daily decisions with commercial and brand positioning reality. If this was your money, how would you spend it? If you're an entrepreneur, chances are this is your money—so tread carefully and don't get distracted! Think FACTS and stats.

2. **Plan like a Visionary** (Shed the blinkers and think big— what's possible?)—Creativity

All companies and commercial operations need a plan, a vision, a why and a way forward. Planning like a visionary allows you to step outside of traditional business constraints and start dreaming. What's possible? Think about where the decisions you make now could take you. What are the forks in the road and the options ahead?

Is there a common goal? Do you have a big-picture perspective to avoid panic and reactionary steps when faced with a challenge?

A strong vision creates culture inside an organisation. It creates the messages that resonate with your customers. It brings to life the brand or the products you offer. It is essential for sustainability, growth and development.

Creativity and connection to great ideas need space and inspiration. Schedule time for inspiration and future planning. If you are thinking on your feet, pause to consider the implications of a decision you're about to recommend or undertake.

3. **Act like a Buddha** (You can be fast but you need to be clear)—Clarity and Calm

Our best decisions are made when we create space to tune into our experience and inner voice. It goes beyond intuition. Call it "tuning in", like finding the right radio station and getting rid of the static. Static is the noise of our subconscious, taking us off course from our knowledge and expertise.

Most people don't create the space to think clearly and with clarity. They make decisions in the spur of the moment.

Take a pause and say, "I'll get back to you," or, "Give me five minutes." If it's an email, don't respond straight away.

Get up, walk away from the computer and change your mental environment. Breathe and listen to your intuition before you reply. This takes the emotion out of your response and you can look at the situation with a fresh perspective.

To wrap this up

As a manager or leader, your actions speak louder than words. The interactions you have with others during challenging circumstances and conversations solidify your credibility. Nothing is so urgent that you can't take two minutes to pause and hit re-boot.

This does not mean you need to be a pushover. In fact, it puts you in a position of strength, consideration and confidence.

No matter what size business you are running or working within, there's a certain harmony to thinking like a CEO (leadership), planning like a visionary (creativity) and the ability to act like a Buddha (clarity and calm).

Take the story out of the situation, step back, lean on your experience and have some faith in yourself and those around you. There is always a solution.

NOTES

HEALTHY | WEALTHY | WISE

Here's my 10 Tips To Keep Momentum and Enjoy the Journey

1. **Be Consistent**

Consistency is key.

Each day you should be doing something that you actually love, enjoy, makes you laugh and is good for you. Think of it as topping up your vitality bank.

It's not about expensive long lunches, big purchase items or taking the whole day out to be reckless—I am more referring to simple routines that ensure you enjoy being present, the work you do and look after the body that you have all at the same time.

Build fitness and wellbeing dates into your weekly planning, and make them transparent in your agenda.

Choose a workout buddy to keep you accountable and meet up with them for at least two sessions per week.

Have a team walk and talk as the huddle or take it outside and have your meetings in a new location.

Book the movies, go on a casual date, call a friend or go try the new cafe around the corner. What ever you can do that breaks the monotony and makes you smile.

CHAPTER 9

THE CONSISTENCY LIST (STUFF I CAN DO, DEMONSTRATE AND ENCOURAGE OTHERS TO DO DAILY):

_____
_____
_____
_____
_____
_____
_____

LIST A FEW IDEAS HERE:

_____
_____
_____
_____
_____
_____
_____
_____
_____

2. **Create A Tangible Corporate Vitality Program—even if it's just you in your business.**

Like personal health and wellbeing, corporate and personal health activities are the first things to go when budgets are tight and teams are stressed.

But when you cut back on what makes you (or your workforce) healthy, your bottom line and performance are hit hard.

There are costs associated with the show-up employee—the person who comes to work every day but is not motivated, does not perform or is sick. This includes entrepreneurs.

If you keep on pushing without a well balanced mindset and approach to your personal healthy stress is going to get in the way of making great decisions.

Stressed-out decision making is dangerous—it's when don't think strategically or with initiative, and instead operate on a fight-or-flight mentality.

- Exhausted employees make mistakes. These mistakes could involve machinery, financial deals, hiring the wrong people, getting into workplace disputes or breaching code of conduct.

CHAPTER 9

Are your current corporate wellbeing and training plans relevant? Is that company health or leadership program getting you and your team a return on investment by increasing engagement, performance and productivity?

Or is it just ticking the health and safety boxes, not tailored to truly fit your industry and operational landscape?

Mental-stress claims are the most expensive form of workers' compensation claim[8], and often result in workers being absent from work for extended periods.

Most businesses run company health and wellbeing programs poorly. Too often, expensive, well-intended programs never truly get off the ground.

The exact same issue applies to entrepreneurs—that buy expensive gym memberships or hire personal trainers and cancel after a while or just stop going.

Are you keeping it simple or getting tangled up in big plans and dramatic statements?

There's' no need to rush out and buy fancy equipment to workout in the office or at home, or suddenly declare a whole new culture for how you work to your clients and colleagues. Good things take time and happen seamlessly with subtle changes and new habits.

- Go back to basics and use your surroundings for your fitness and meetings and look at how you set your office up as well.
- How can you be more efficient
- What can make it more inspiring
- Where is there an element of a personal touch, a sense of energy and vitality to where you work and how you work.

Have an issue finding even a spare second for yourself—the REALLY look at your agenda and ask yourself is that meeting, call, email, distraction absolutely necessary or can I just focus on the core elements for now.

Keep starting new projects before you have finished core products and deliverables that were crucial to this quarter.

There are 10 Great Reasons Why You Need a Corporate Health and Wellbeing Plan[9]

I. Decreased health care cost
II. Work place morale
III. Reduced absenteeism
IV. Reduced overall costs
V. Increased productivity
VI. Increased responsibility
VII. Increased company loyalty
VIII. Reduced sick leaves
IX. Improved work performance
X. Decreased health insurance costs

3. Adopt the 1% Rule

Can't find an hour a day for exercise or to go and meet a good friend for lunch? No worries, find 15 minutes and start from there.

Functional fitness, using your own body weight, yoga-style stretching and skipping all help to create a toned and fit physique. And they add diversity to your fitness routine to keep things interesting.

- Pick up the phone and have a conversation instead of texting
- Book a coffee or quick post work catch up in the early evening
- You don't need a gym, an extensive regime or a massive reason to reconnect with your fitness, your friends or your family throughout the day.
- Start looking at your agenda differently and how you can use 15 minutes to mix things up.

"YOU WILL NEVER HAVE MORE TIME THAN YOU DO RIGHT NOW."

NIKKI FOGDEN-MOORE

4. Involve Others: Engage family, colleagues and friends

Being a leader can be a lonely game—however when you understand that ultimate leadership is across all areas of your life it becomes easier to involve others and allow yourself a sustainable approach that seamlessly with both business and personal.

There is a point where you don't need to bring your business home with you and vice versa—but we should be an extension of ourselves where ever we are. Compartmentalising too much can be stressful and create anxiety, lack of authenticity and constant negotiation between yourself and your surroundings.

Be present where you are—but understand that there are qualities you have that serve you in both worlds and life becomes much easier, balanced and in harmony when we can be ourselves consistently.

Make family, colleagues and friends a part of your plan. This will make your new approach enjoyable, rather than just another idea that never actually comes to fruition.

For example if creating a consistent fitness regime is part of your 90-day plan then find some workout buddies and get strength in numbers.

Ask your direct reports or people you work with to nominate a fun group fitness challenge you can all work towards.

Schedule meetings and catch ups with people you know well while you workout or do something active.

According to the Department of Kinesiology at Indiana University, people are 94% more likely to stick to their workout when they make a date to train with someone else.

5. Listen to your body—Get Off Autopilot

A key element of leading yourself and others is inner wisdom and knowing when to relax, listen to your body and get the best out of your day.

How well do you know yourself by now.

Are you a morning or an evening person. What foods give you energy and what foods make you feel sluggish and uncomfortable after eating. What you fuel your body with is crucial for mental and physical wellbeing.

What situations at work or in the office instantly stress you out, where do your strengths lie in dealing with issues.

"TAKE THE TIME
TO FULLY DEVELOP AND
ENJOY THE JOURNEY
ALONG THE WAY."

TONY ROBBINS

6. <u>Sleep</u>

Ongoing sleep deficiency is linked to an increased risk of heart disease, kidney disease, high-blood pressure, diabetes and stroke. Lack of sleep lowers our immune system, reduces our judgement and can be a personal and performance liability at work, as well as at home.

If you are tired, relax. Time a moment out to recharge rather than pushing through it and putting your body under more stress.

Switching off is just as crucial as being switched on. Most importantly, you don't need to spend an hour every day to reboot your hard drive. With the right approach, it can take just a few minutes to recalibrate.

When we get tired, we don't make great decisions. Stress levels increase, our chemical make-up changes into a more acidic environment. Stress and lack of rest are the leading contributors of workplace burnout. Sleep is a basic human need. If you run your day on high octane without rest, chances are your evening sleep will be restless and limited.

7. <u>Have Fun—It's Allowed. Do something you LOVE—OFTEN!</u>

When did we stop having fun as adults?

Do things that make your heart sing. You can run, walk, do yoga, join a gym, play football with your kids. Read, travel more, network, book your favourite restaurants or just hibernate.

Whatever activities you do, they should be for YOU.

Success comes from combining what you love to do with what you are good at.

It is amazing how bringing a bit of fun into your life can quickly create tangible results. Refresh your health, wellness and social outlook to keep the spark alive and enjoy the journey.

Have Adventures

When is the last time you did something spontaneous?

I'm forever having adventures. This does not mean that I am void a sense of responsibility or not delivering on my work—it just means that I know I love to say yes to new things, travel to new places and continue to evolve and explore.

When we open our world with new experiences we open our minds and hearts as leaders as well. Live a little.

8. Be Travel Fit

Exercise is not location dependent. Whether you need to spend a week on the road, attend a conference or continually travel interstate for business, there are simple ways for you to integrate fitness into your travel schedule.

Take your gym with you:

- It's easier than you may think. Use body-weight exercises and pack some basic, lightweight items and a pair of running shoes.
- Stock your mental hard drive with exercises you can do anywhere, and download your favourite videos and fitness apps to your iPad or tablet to keep you on track.

Back to basics:

- Create time in the mornings to get some fresh air before you start your meetings.
- Swap your heels or business shoes for trainers and explore your new surroundings on foot or by bike.
- It's also the perfect way to get your bearings (and find the best coffee or juice spots!)

15-minute express session:

- A quick walk or jog, followed by a super set of 25 push-ups, 25 crunches, 25 tricep dips and 25 prisoner squats.
- Finish with three yoga poses to stretch.

Skip your way fit:

- A skipping rope will roll up and fit inside your shoe. Skip as a warm up and cool down at different tempos, adding core work and body-weight exercises in between.
- You'll be surprised how effective skipping is for agility and cardio conditioning.
- I like to do a skipping session beside roof-top pools or places with a great garden and view.
- It's an awesome fresh-air session and you can start your day feeling like Rocky!

Use the on-site gym or pool:

- Research where you are staying and find out what facilities are available. Pack your swim goggles and squeeze in a few laps between meals and other activities.

Pack suspension straps:

- I always take these on trips of four days or more. It ensures I can train on the spot for just 15 minutes a day, or longer when combined with cardio.

Use nature as your gym:

- Embrace your surroundings.
- If you're in an island paradise or near the beach, head to the water for your workouts. If you're in the countryside or even in a city that has amazing parks, explore the environment by hiking, running, walking or biking.
- If you're away on a retreat and feeling adventurous, you could even try horse riding. Why not?!

9. <u>Digital Detox—Disconnect to Reconnect</u>

Taking regular breaks from your laptop, phone, tablet and TV can rapidly produce great results. Quick digital detoxes can:

- Reduce the effects of dry eyes and strained vision.
- Create a pause of mental clarity and creativity.
- Reconnect you with your surroundings and purpose.
- Help you make informed decisions rather than reactionary ones.
- Help you notice your posture and breathing.
- Improve sleep.
- Reduce stress.
- Increase mental and physical vitality.

During the day, place a sticky note on your computer that says "take a nano break" to remind you to get up and walk away from your computer. Also, stay off Facebook and social media in the morning on the way to work. Listen to music, a podcast or read a book instead.

Take a fresh-air break at lunch time minus your phone and iPad. Look up, look around. If you're at home, take the dog for a walk or do something active with your kids.

- Use time away from work to re-charge your mental and physical batteries. Avoid television, illuminated alarm clocks and other digital stimuli in the bedroom. Instead of watching TV or working late on the computer, read a book before you go to sleep. Meditate and concentrate on breathing.

Think of a digital detox as recharging your own batteries. If we do not fully recharge our batteries, we diminish our energy levels and ability to handle stress and daily tasks. Sometimes, you need to disconnect to reconnect.

If you're pushing yourself and not listening to your body, chances are you're going to get a nasty wake-up call—one you could have avoided.

My suggestion is to use the power of pause—or what I call the "nano break" approach. It's an incredible gift to be able to log off for mini moments throughout the day so you can look after your body, mind and soul.

Here's some nano break ideas:

Mini Mindfulness Moments:

- Set reminders on your computer to take a nano break so you can step away from your screen.
- Go talk to someone in another department instead of sending an email.
- Grab a glass of water or go for a stroll as you work on creative ideas and problem solving.
- Do some subtle stretching, even!

Meditation in the office is very 'in' right now too. Relaxation and yoga aides in releasing the molecule GABA which slows down the firing of neurons and creates a sense of calmness, naturally.

Ditch the lift: Use stairs and don't take a taxi to meetings around the corner.

Be posture aware: Using your core is not just something you do at the gym. Pull your belly button to your spine while you are working, standing, walking and talking. It's a constant way to work your abs and no one will notice

Use a stand-up work desk: If you feel you need to stay glued to your computer, then work while standing up and take regular breaks. You're more likely to walk over to your colleague to talk to them rather than send an email when you use a stand-up work station.

10. Walk and Talks:

The Best Decisions can be Made Out of the Office or on the Move.

According to research company Atlassian, US businesses reported a salary cost of $37 billion due to unnecessary meetings. They also found that:

- 91% of people daydreamed during meetings
- 96% missed meetings
- 39% slept during a meeting
- 45% of people felt overwhelmed by the number of meetings they attended, putting them behind their usual work and placing them under constant pressure

Walking meetings have long been the go-to for the ultra-successful. Steve Jobs, the late founder of Apple, Facebook's Mark Zuckerberg and Jack Dorsey of Twitter have all been known to conduct walking meetings. It's time more business leaders embraced this clever and efficient use of time.

You need to shift your approach to meetings. Get people out of the board room. Get your team to step outside or even walk the corridors to give them a fresh perspective and create a renewed sense of energy and purpose. Not only will you be able to solve ideas faster, you will gain a sense of connection to the people in your team.

Grab some fresh air to discuss key topics, then come back and write up the key points. You could even go for a stroll along the corridors.

Here are five key benefits to walk and talks:

Fresh oxygen to your brain.

Movement is essential for healthy brain function. Any role within an organisation requires the person be switched on. Walking results in fresh, oxygenated blood throughout the body. A healthy body and healthy mind go hand in hand. From a neurochemical perspective, our brains are more relaxed during walks due to the release of certain chemicals like dopamine, the reward molecule that makes you feel great when you have done, achieved sensed something positive or pleasurable, Serotonin:the Confidence Molecule and interestingly enough GABA: "The Anti-Anxiety Molecule".

All of this interesting scientific and extremely important information can be found in the Journal of Complementary Medicine and various other medical journals and publications. In case you want to delve into this further.

Fresh perspective.

Great leaders do not determine their success by the number of hours they sit in meetings, but by their understanding of the physical and metaphorical company landscape. Being on the move enables you to "check in" with your organisation's vibe. You will have increased awareness of small issues, which could lead to larger problems if not resolved.

Walk and talks will give you a better understanding of your staff and the environment they operate in.

CHAPTER 9

Best use of time.

Walk and talks promote clearer, faster meetings, as generally you won't be writing things down until you get back for a regroup. A nano break on the go to chew through an idea with a colleague can save hours of meeting times, and provide a new way of looking at an issue or project.

Walk and talks are short, sharp and combine business vitality with personal vitality.

Relationship building and engagement = visibility and connection.

Being seen and connecting with your staff is crucial for authentic leadership. Hiding yourself away in the corner office is not going to achieve real teamwork and initiative.

According to the Harvard Business Review, the act of walking as we talk leads to increased creative thinking, more productivity and connection between employees.

Allows you to lead by example.

Walk and talks enable you to work on your personal wellbeing, as well as the wellbeing of your business and staff. Lead by example and encourage all levels of management to do walk and talks with their teams.

Remember to set boundaries. A walk and talk doesn't mean a two-hour lunch. And bear in mind that highly confidential information is best kept in private environments. Be aware of others working as you conduct a meeting on the move.

Above all else, be consistent. Your teams will trust this is an "everyday culture" when they see you regularly getting up from your desk to conduct meetings on the go.

"SOME MEN
DREAM OF WORTH
ACCOMPLISHMENTS
WHILE OTHERS
STAY AWAKE
AND DO THEM."

NIKKI FOGDEN-MOORE

HEALTHY | WEALTHY | WISE

Plan To Be An Awesome Leader In All Areas of Life

Focusing on a fantastic business is great. However, planning your own personal finance, budgets, development, admin and use of time is also crucial to living a more harmonious life.

> *Warren Buffet once said that the first thing anyone with a positive approach to money should do is check their bank balance every morning and every evening. You must keep your personal finances and wealth top of mind.*

Look to excel in a balanced manner that includes knowing your personal finances just as well as the runnings of the business.

Consider how grow your worldly experience—your inner wisdom and connection as well as your expertise for your work, business or career.

Just as your company or board does, you should review your role every two to three years. Look up and assess where your strengths lie.

What personal and professional development would be worthwhile undertaking? Do you still love what you do?

> *When we combine what we are good at with what we enjoy doing, the results are doubled. Know that your skills, your strengths, your expertise and what motivates you all go hand in hand. The more you love what you do, you do what you love.*

Why leave bills, invoices, tax and accounts until the last minute? Working weekly on your admin, productivity and personal finance allows you to keep your finger on the pulse of your own planning.

Always know your bank balance, your costs and what's coming up. Being prepared and great in the boardroom should extend to your own balance sheet at home.

Today's corporate climate for roles, responsibilities and job prospects moves much faster than 10 years ago. What we used to plan for in five to seven years now often happens in as little as two years. This includes career development and promotion, and depends on the type of job you have and the industry you are in.

Do you have a succession plan—for you, for those in your team to step up?

You cannot expect someone else to come along and give you a succession plan. Whether it's branching out on your own, accepting board of director roles, handing your business over to a family member or just understanding whether or not your business enables your lifestyle, you require a proper five to 10-year grow-and-exit strategy.

If you've got a few minutes now here's some key questions to think about for personal admin and future proofing.

A Fitpreneur's approach is not one of auto pilot. Know your path, your skills, your experience and your expertise.

HEALTHY | WEALTHY | WISE

NOTES

CHAPTER 9

NOTES

BEFORE YOU GO...

Sending You Off With Your Super Leader Powers

Often, the biggest barriers to achieving energy, harmony and sustainable success in our lives are our pre-conceived ideas about "how things should go".

We tell ourselves stories about how the day should go, how many hours we should be at the office and what exercise should look like. That's a lot of pressure that's not based on facts at all—just assumptions and old mindsets. What will happen after you put this book down.

Be accountable, be transparent. Re-assess your goals and your day-to-day time allocation regularly.

Get out of your own way. You now have a fresh perspective.

Throw out the preconceptions about work life balance, giving one thing up for the other. You know it's not sustainable and won't create lasting results. You now have the work/life BLEND. The role of being healthy, wealthy and wise.

Our personality, skills, knowledge and positive approach need to shine through in the boardroom and at home. To ensure this, you need to:

- Review your personal and wellbeing goals every 90 days, as you do with your business.
- Make family time and fitness priorities in your agenda.
- Be clear about your priorities without grand gestures— consistency is key.
- Lead by example.

As you set out on the next part of your journey, leading in business and in life remember that it takes enormous energy and fortitude to build businesses, bring projects to life and create something meaningful.

It's not the space around us but the space we create in our minds that truly counts.

Everyday work harder on yourself more than anything else. You can then give more to others, do more, create more and provide more than you could ever imagine. To be the ultimate leader we must master the art of blending healthy, wealthy and wise.

I hope this book has given you the kick start to the next level living and leadership you need to make that a reality.

Nikki

5 AWESOME POINTS I WANT TO TAKE AWAY FROM THIS BOOK RIGHT NOW

About The Author

Nikki Fogden-Moore is the Ultimate Vitality Expert. She specialises in coaching high achievers to bring business and personal vitality to life, to engage in next-level thinking to create harmony and purpose.

She runs tailored corporate vitality programs, writes regularly for several business magazines, was the head trainer for Women's Health & Fitness Magazine for more than four years, and has been running leadership workshops and private retreats for more than a decade internationally.

You can reach Nikki via her website www.nikkifogdenmoore.com, by emailing nikki@nikkifogdenmoore.com or on social media @nfogdenmoore.

OTHER BOOKS BY NIKKI
Visit www.nikkifogdenmoore.com/store and available on Amazon

MINI GUIDES
The Wake Up Workout™
The 1% Rule
Digital Detox
Finding Your Why

Endnotes

1. Price Waterhouse Coopers Research 2015
2. Health and Fitness Revolution interview 2016
3. psychology.org.au/pyschologyweek/survey
4. Stress In America survey, conducted by Harris Poll
5. Anna Johansson, Published April 2016
6. Note the 90-day plan sheet is available for download or you can use the one in the book. Just check at the resources section for the links too.
7. Published November 2015
8. Forbes 2015
9. Wellness Quotes

The Niktionary and Resources

The 3 Pillars Of Leadership
https://www.nikkifogdenmoore.com/podcasts/radical-self-belief-the-mojo-maker-podcast/episodes/2147556198

90-day Plan
https://www.nikkifogdenmoore.com/podcasts/radical-self-belief-the-mojo-maker-podcast/episodes/2147556197

Winning Week
https://www.nikkifogdenmoore.com/blog/tmm147-how-to-master-winning-weeks

Winning Week Podcast Episode
https://www.nikkifogdenmoore.com/podcasts/radical-self-belief-the-mojo-maker-podcast/episodes/2147556232

The Vitality Road Map
https://www.nikkifogdenmoore.com/podcasts/radical-self-belief-the-mojo-maker-podcast/episodes/2147556211

Finding Your Why with Layne Beachley
https://www.nikkifogdenmoore.com/podcasts/radical-self-belief-the-mojo-maker-podcast/episodes/2147556233

Accountability with Trevor Hendy
https://www.nikkifogdenmoore.com/podcasts/radical-self-belief-the-mojo-maker-podcast/episodes/2147556250

Mindsense with Mike Duff
https://www.nikkifogdenmoore.com/podcasts/radical-self-belief-the-mojo-maker-podcast/episodes/2147556238

'Excitimin8ting' - just a term i use when things are especially fantastic.

My Mantra—Think Like A CEO, Plan Like A Visionary,
Act Like A Buddha

Giving Back Episode 50
https://www.nikkifogdenmoore.com/podcasts/radical-self-belief-the-mojo-maker-podcast/episodes/2147556204

Note some URL's may change due to website updates. If you cannot get a direct link please head to www.nikkifogdenmoore.com and type the key word or subject into the search area.

References and Resources

Values list and tips and considerations mindtools.com

The Layne Beachley Aim For The Stars Foundation
www.aimforthestars.com.au

Huffington Post articles huffingtonpost.com and http://www.huffingtonpost.com.au/2015/11/07/australians-report-finances-are-causing-most-stress-in-life/

Workplace Stress http://www.forbes.com/sites hbsworkingknowledge/2015/01/26/workplace-stress-responsible-for-up-to-190-billion-in-annual-u-s-heathcarecosts/#74eeede43332 Michael Blanding

The 7 Biggest Challenges That Small Business Owners Face in 2016 Anna Johansson http://www.inc.com/anna-johansson/the-7-biggest-challenges-thatsmall-business-owners-face-in-2016.html

The American Institute of Stress

10 Challenges that CEOs Will Face in 2016 http://www.businessnewsdaily.com/3625-new-year-challenges.html Brittney Helmrich

Psychology Week http://www.psychology.org.au psychologyweek/survey/

http://www.wellnessquotes.com/top10-reasons-why-your-company-needs-anemployee-wellness-program.html

http://workplaceinfo.com.au/ohs/safety-in-the-workplace/analysis/stressed,-depressed-and-unhappy-at-work-report#.Vc90OV97cc

Journal of Complementary Medicine

Atlassian

Harvard Business Review

Wellness Quotes http://www.wellnessquotes.com/top10-reasons-why-yourcompany-needs-an-employee-wellness-program.html

Source: 30 CEOs Reveal the Daily Habits Responsible for Their Success http://www.inc.com/christina-desmarais/30-ceos-reveal-the-daily-habits-responsible-fortheir-success.html

NOTES

www.ingramcontent.com/pod-product-compliance
Lightning Source LLC
Chambersburg PA
CBHW050610300426
44112CB00013B/2150